A Treasure's Trove

Puzzle Book Companion 2

101 NEW!
Puzzles,
Clues,
Maps,
Tantalizing Tales,
and Stories
of Real Treasure

Treasure Trove, Inc.
NEW CANAAN, CT

Bruce Park, Greenwich, Connecticut, built on the site of two unsolved train robberies.

A Treasure's Trove

Puzzle Book Companion 2

101 NEW!
Puzzles,
Clues,
Maps,
Tantalizing Tales,
and Stories
of Real Treasure

Treasure Trove, Inc.
New Canaan, CT

Treasure Trove, Inc.

Published in the United States by
Treasure Trove, Inc.
161 Cherry Street
New Canaan, CT 06840

Distributed by Simon Scribbles
an imprint of Simon & Schuster, Inc.
1230 Avenue of the Americas
New York, NY 10020

Visit www.atreasurestrove.com and www.alchemistdar.com
for more information about the treasure hunts and the next book.

Manufactured in the United States of America

2 4 6 8 10 9 7 5 3 1

ISBN-13: 978-0-9760618-6-1
ISBN-10: 0-9760618-6-4

First Edition

Contents

INTRODUCTION

Treasure hunting can be an illusive pastime. The search requires looking for clues that have been ingeniously hidden. In many cases, the treasure has been long forgotten, relegated to the dustbins of history and legend. And if the treasure wasn't forgotten, odds are that someone has gone and claimed it for themselves long ago.

Sometimes clues are so obvious that people overlook them. Consider, for example, a story I heard about Captain Kidd's buried treasure. Nearly every state in the Northeastern U.S. has several tales about how Captain Kidd buried his pirate loot on a dark and stormy night. I've compiled many such stories for the book you now hold. But one story in particular mentions Captain Kidd coming ashore on the Connecticut River near Glastonbury, Connecticut. Anyone with a map can learn that one of the roads in the area has a curious name: Dug Road. Might this road have been named for something buried and then dug up? Maybe it was a road that required a lot of digging during construction. Either way, this dichotomy is exactly the kind of mystery that has fascinated me ever since my early childhood, when I dug up my grandmother's backyard looking for buried treasure.

I'm convinced that there are hundreds, or perhaps thousands, of similar stories out there, waiting for inquisitive people to come along and ask the right questions. I wrote this book to get you excited about treasure and treasure hunting. I also wrote it to get you thinking about how to solve the puzzles in my fairy tale, *A Treasure's Trove*, and its sequel, *Secrets of the Alchemist Dar*.

Both books are sweet stories about Forest Creatures, a handsome woodcarver and his beautiful wife, and their encounters with good fairies and bad fairies. But the books are also more than just fairy tales; they are quests.

Hidden in the story and illustrations of *A Treasure's Trove* are clues to find real treasure. Once found, these tokens can be used to claim more than $1,000,000 in gold, platinum, and jewels. Now that nearly all of the treasures from the first book have been found, I'm preparing a treasure hunt of much larger proportion. All of the puzzles will be right there in the pages of my next book, *Secrets of the Alchemist Dar*. But the clues won't be easy, and I'm raising the stakes. This time, instead of hiding only a few tokens, I'm preparing a hunt for one hundred rings around the world.

Many people will tell you that treasure doesn't exist and that looking for it is a fantasy, a waste of time. They'll also tell you that adults don't read fairy tales. Both statements are false.

I created *A Treasure's Trove* so that everyone could experience the thrill of the hunt. Now I'm ready for another adventure. Even if you don't find my treasure—and believe me, it is very real—I hope you have a wonderful time searching for it.

Michael Stadther

HOW TO USE THIS BOOK

I intended this puzzle book as a companion to *A Treasure's Trove* and its sequel, *Secrets of the Alchemist Dar*. Some puzzles and illusions will point you directly to techniques that I used to hide clues in both of my fairy tales. Others may simply give you a new way of looking at the world and at logic.

Don't worry if you can't solve some of the puzzles—not solving one won't lessen your chances of finding the real treasure in the fairy tales.

I hope you'll share the stories, puzzles and illusions in this book with your family or your children. Most of them are appropriate for people of all ages. Regardless of whether or not you think you're a puzzle person, approach them with an open mind. And don't get frustrated if you can't solve the puzzles right away. Putting up mental roadblocks won't help to accomplish anything. The solutions, in most cases, are obvious, hidden in plain sight. The secret is not to read too much into them, but to open your mind to all possibilities.

For example, can you see a word in the shapes below?

Look at it carefully. I promise that it is not difficult and it's right before your eyes. Most people can't see it right away, but once you stop looking at the shapes and look at the space between them you may see the word: Trover. (If, however, you still don't see it, the answer is at the bottom of the next page.)

It was there all along—right in front you! It was completely obvious. But in the beginning, most people simply don't know how to interpret what their eyes are telling them. This puzzle book won't guarantee that you will find the jewels that I have hidden. But it will get you thinking like a treasure hunter.

I've also included some stories about real treasures around the world. These are stories that have been part of treasure lore for many years and they are all very real.

Finally, I've included a little information about ciphers. Ciphers are ways of concealing the meaning of written information from all but the author of the information.

While the cipher section may be a little too complex for some people, you should at least figure out that the map to a treasure may be written in a language that only the person who hides the treasure can understand—and you may have to do a little work to decipher the clues.

But no matter whether you find one of the treasures or not, the best way to use this book is to have fun reading about treasures and solving the puzzles.

Several bodies of water in New York's Adirondack region were named for Moses Follensby, an enigmatic hermit rumored to have buried a fortune in gold near Tupper Lake.

TREASURE STORIES

In the quest for land and wealth, hundreds of brash adventurers either triumphed or failed in the harsh terrain of the American West. One of these treasure seekers was fabled California pioneer Peter Lassen, a prospector who died under mysterious circumstances.

FATHER OF LASSEN COUNTY
PETER LASSEN

Born in 1800 in Farum, Denmark, a village near Copenhagen, Lassen left Denmark for America in 1830. He arrived in Boston, later moved to Philadelphia, then to Keytesville, Missouri. A blacksmith by trade, he remained in Missouri until 1839, when he joined a band heading west to Oregon. Once there, he boarded a ship and sailed down the West Coast, eventually traveling to Sacramento, then a part of Mexico.

Lassen sought and obtained Mexican citizenship, which allowed him to own property, and was granted five Spanish leagues (22,000 acres) near Deer Creek, 140 miles north of Sacramento. Envisioning a future as a prosperous landlord, he established Bosquejo Ranch and nearby Benton City. He returned to Missouri in 1847 to recruit settlers for his new community, which at the time was the northernmost settlement in California. The following spring, Lassen accompanied a small group of emigrants over the perilous Lassen Trail, only to find that most of Benton City's population became part of the gold rush and relocated to seek their fortunes elsewhere.

In 1850, a series of financial problems forced Lassen to sell his ranch on Deer Creek. Later that year, he failed to find gold in northeastern California but struck it rich five years later in Honey Lake Valley in the northern Sierra Nevada mountains.

During his time in Honey Lake Valley, Lassen served as territory president and also became a surveyor. Then, in 1858, when news circulated of a silver deposit in Nevada's Black Rock Desert, Lassen organized an ill-fated prospecting party. He divided his expedition into two groups, with the intention of meeting at Black Rock. His own three-man group arrived first. Then, on April 26, 1859,

Northern California

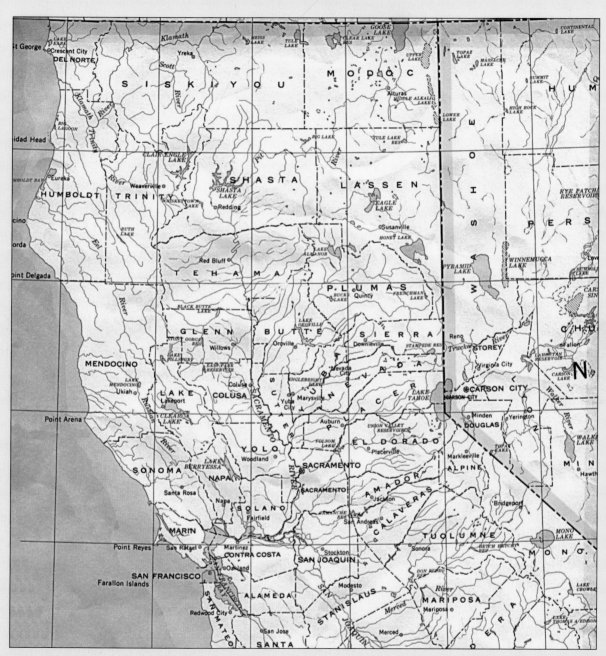

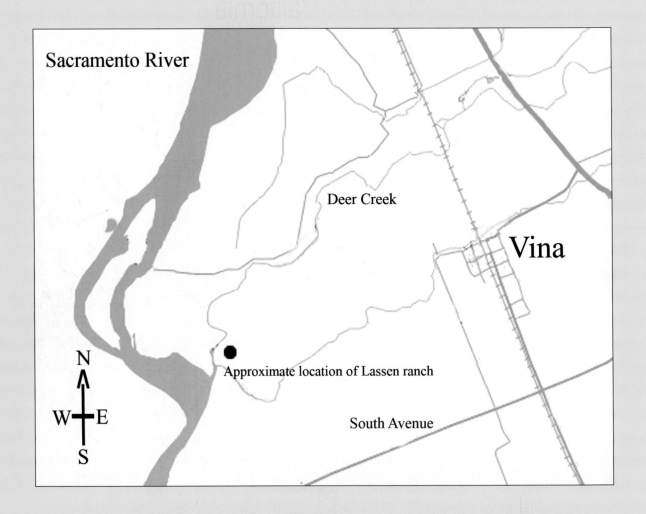

Sacramento River

Deer Creek

Vina

Approximate location of Lassen ranch

N
W — E
S

South Avenue

two shots shattered the early morning silence: The first killed one of Lassen's companions; the second killed Lassen. The third member of Lassen's group, Lemericus Wyatt, survived to relay the tale and claimed the men were attacked by Indians. However, many historians have remained skeptical of Wyatt's story.

Was Lassen murdered by Indians? Or did Wyatt, working alone or with others, conspire to murder Lassen? Some years before his death, Lassen is thought to have buried gold coins and gold dust, either near his home at the confluence of Deer Creek and the Sacramento River at Vina, or along the Lassen Trail, which follows Deer Creek. If it was buried near his ranch, Lassen may have moved his gold before he sold the property. Perhaps someone else knew the location of his hoard, killed him, and secretly retrieved it.

Nearly twenty years after Lassen's death, a miner named Obe Leininger found a ledge of gold-flecked quartz somewhere in Deer Creek Canyon. Thinking the location might have been the source of Lassen's fabled treasure, Leininger hid his pick in the trunk of a nearby tree. Returning later, the miner was unable to find it. He spent the rest of his life searching for the ledge, alone and with others. But he never saw the ledge again. Perhaps it is still there, as the story goes, forty miles from Chico, somewhere to the left of State Highway 32. There, just beyond Deer Creek, between the mouth of Calf Creek and the Potato Patch campground maintained by the U.S. Forest Service, treasure hunters have looked for Lassen's gold mine for nearly 150 years.

Much of Nevada's Black Rock Desert, where pioneer Peter Lassen met his demise, is now under the jurisdiction of the Bureau of Land Management, part of the U.S. Department of the Interior.

The source of Lassen's gold appears to have been lost to history, but maybe his treasure is still waiting to be found, buried somewhere on his old ranch.

Moses Follensby

Little is known about Moses Follensby, an enigmatic hermit whose legacy is remembered in the names of several lakes in New York's Adirondack region, near Brighton, in Franklin County. Follensby moved to the wilderness around 1820, building a log cabin with one window on a three-mile-long pond southeast of the present-day village of Tupper Lake. He spent most of his time trapping and fishing.

Those who knew Captain Follensby, as he was sometimes called, claimed he was a disgruntled English nobleman and a former English army officer. He also is reported to have possessed a treasure of gold and silver coins worth $400,000, which he buried near his cabin.

Sunset in the Adirondacks, Upstate New York.

But where was his cabin? Writings from the period indicate that he built a rough-hewn log house in the rear of a "blunt headland." The lake itself was described as having five or six bays, no islands, and a brook running into the lake at the north end. All of these features are present in Follensby Pond, a body of water near Tupper Lake. Two other lakes in the area share Follensby's name, a fact which has confounded treasure hunters for more than one hundred years, but neither of those lakes has the geographic features described in the treasure stories.

Follensby disappeared in 1823. No one knows where he was buried. But at least one story suggested he died of fever. Shortly before Follensby's death, a sportsman and a trapper happened by his cabin. Hearing shouts, the two forced their way inside. Follensby was lying on a bed of bear skins, deathly ill. The pair stayed with him through the night while he ranted deliriously about battles and a woman named Georgiana. He spoke of a chest, pointing repeatedly toward his stone fireplace. In the morning Follensby died. The visitors wrapped him in the bear skins, buried him, and marked his grave with two simple stones. Then they started looking for Follensby's treasure.

The visitors soon found a chest hidden under a hearthstone. Inside were a jewel-encrusted sword and a gold scabbard, along with a pair of richly fashioned silver pistols inlaid with pearl. They also found a dressing case decorated with gold and jewels. It contained gold and bejeweled toiletries, a British uniform, a gold-laced hat, and a stack of letters. They put their find back in the chest, removed the valuables to their boat, and departed to spend the night in a hunter's shanty some miles away. When they awoke the next morning, the chest was gone.

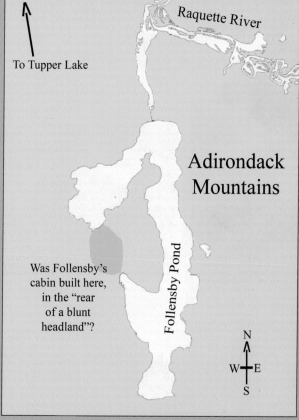

No one knows who took the chest or what happened to its contents. And no one has ever claimed to have located Follensby's fabled cache. Treasure hunters, hoping to find his lost fortune, have been trying to learn the exact location of Follensby's cabin for more than one hundred years. If found today, his treasure would be worth much more than $400,000. Perhaps it is still there. Or maybe it never existed.

Yet another account from the period suggests Follensby was a French marquis who was wounded at the Battle of Waterloo. Although the stories differ in their explanations of his origin, both maintain that Follensby disappeared around the same time. The truth may never be known.

Sometimes called the Robin Hood of the West, legendary outlaw Butch Cassidy helped to orchestrate one of the longest strings of successful bank and train robberies in American history. The oldest of thirteen children, he was born in Beaver, Utah, in 1866. His parents, Mormon pioneers who emigrated from England, named him Robert LeRoy Parker.

Butch spent his early years on his parents' homestead in Circleville, Utah. During his teens, he worked on ranches across western Utah. But things didn't go well for the family business. Young Roy, as he was known at the time, soon acquired a distaste for the law. He fell under the influence of Mike Cassidy, a disreputable rancher who became his mentor. Then his father lost land to another homesteader in a property-rights dispute. By 1884, Roy began using the name Butch Cassidy and had started rustling cattle on a regular basis.

Butch's travels took him to Telluride, Colorado, but he soon became familiar with an area to the west known as Robbers' Roost, a vast canyonland in the foothills of Utah's Henry Mountains. Then, in 1889, Butch and three other cowboys committed their first major crime. After careful planning, a trait that would become a hallmark of Butch's later heists, the group robbed the San Miguel Valley Bank in Telluride, riding off with more than $20,000. They retreated to Brown's Hole, a hideout along the Green River near the Utah–Wyoming border, before moving north to Lander, Wyoming.

At a time when cattle barons were putting smaller ranchers out of business, Butch's preference for stealing herds from larger ranchers cemented his reputation as an outlaw fighting for settlers' rights. But the law caught up with him in Wyoming. He was nabbed with a stolen herd in 1894 and spent a year and a half in a dark prison in Laramie.

After his release, Butch headed straight for Brown's Hole, where he became associated with a gang who called themselves the Wild Bunch. The group had several well-known members, including Harry Longabaugh, better known as the Sundance Kid, and Harvey Logan, alias Kid Curry. The Wild Bunch took to cattle rustling along the Arizona–Utah border. Then they robbed a bank in Montpelier, Idaho, where they made off with $7,000.

The gang's exploits became increasingly daring, followed by ingenious getaways. After stealing an $8,800 payroll in Price Canyon, Utah, the group outraced a posse using a series of cached horses. Using a strategy learned from the Comanche, the Wild Bunch rode hard for hours, abandoning their tired horses at preplanned locations and then replacing them with fresh mounts.

The group robbed more than a dozen banks and trains between 1896 and 1901. But their success, and subsequent cockiness, contributed to their downfall. During a visit to Fort Worth, Texas, five of the men posed for a photo in suits and derby hats. Pleased with his image, the photographer hung the print in his display window the next day. It promptly caught the eye of an agent with the Pinkerton National Detective Agency, who made sure their likenesses became known to lawmen across the West.

Taken in Fort Worth, Texas, this photograph allowed authorities to intensify their search for the Wild Bunch. From left: Harry Longabaugh, alias the Sundance Kid; William Carver, alias News Carver; Ben Kilpatrick, alias the Tall Texan; Harvey Logan, alias Kid Curry; and Robert LeRoy Parker, alias Butch Cassidy.

Hotly pursued by authorities, the Wild Bunch disbanded by 1902. Butch and the Sundance Kid fled to Europe, then Argentina, where they bought a ranch and attempted to go legit. They eventually returned to robbing banks and trains, this time in South America.

By most accounts, the duo met their demise at the hands of Bolivian soldiers in 1908 or 1909. However, some historians, as well as surviving members of Butch's immediate family, have since claimed the outlaw returned to the United States years later, settling in Spokane, Washington, where he died in 1937. Some say Butch ended his days as a trapper and prospector. Others claim he became an entrepreneur, went bankrupt, and repeatedly visited Wyoming, Utah, and Colorado searching for cash stashed years earlier. One thing is certain: Even today, the legend of Butch Cassidy lives on.

Brown's Park

Straddling northeastern Utah, north-western Colorado, and south-central Wyoming, Brown's Park is an isolated valley, thirty-five miles long and six miles wide. In the days when it was known as Brown's Hole, its location made it an ideal place for anyone who didn't want to be found. It had good land for grazing—a boon for cattle rustlers moving herds from north to south along the fabled Outlaw Trail—and it offered many options for people looking to quickly leave one jurisdiction for another.

Did Butch Cassidy and the Wild Bunch stash loot in the Utah canyonlands? No one knows for sure.

Brown's Hole became a favorite hide-out for Butch Cassidy and the Wild Bunch. The gang repeatedly fled to Brown's Hole. While there, the gang is widely believed to have stashed large amounts of cash in Brown's Hole, including one hoard said to contain $50,000 in gold coins and nuggets. Another account claimed the gang at one time stashed a treasure worth $28,000 at a cabin in the area. No one knows how much of this treasure they managed to recover.

Butch's girlfriend, Josie Morris, lived in Brown's Hole on the Bassett Ranch where Butch is known to have worked; Josie's cabin is still standing. There are remnants of Doc Parson's cabin, where Butch may have lived for a brief time. But most of the visible evidence from those days has long since faded into obscurity.

Skilled at evading lawmen, Butch and the gang had many hideouts, including Robbers' Roost, a canyon-riddled and inhospitable location in south-eastern Utah, and the legendary place known as the Hole-in-the-Wall in south-central Wyoming. All together, these three locations form a line, north to south, roughly two hundred miles as the crow flies. It's entirely possible the robbers stashed loot at all three locations, but most of the treasure stories surrounding Butch Cassidy seem to concentrate on Brown's Hole.

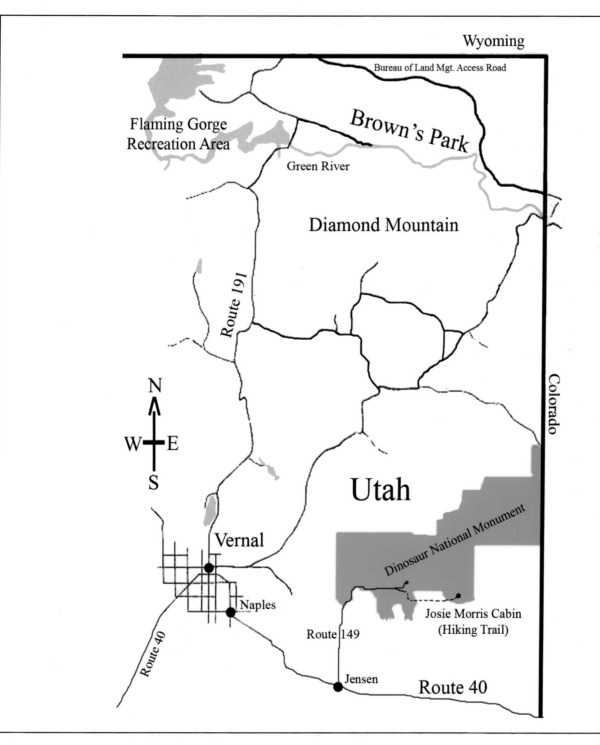

Buried treasure has been a popular theme of pirate fiction. In reality, Captain William Kidd is one of the only pirates known to have buried his loot. On the run from authorities in 1699, he hid at least part of his wealth on Gardiner's Island, located near the tip of Long Island, New York, perhaps intending to use it as a bargaining chip in exchange for his life.

Shortly after Kidd's arrest, British authorities sought the help of John Gardiner, who aided them in retrieving gold and other treasure worth 10,000 British pounds from his island. Kidd insisted that he had hidden treasure worth 40,000 pounds on Gardiner's Island and elsewhere. If there were indeed other caches, Kidd took the knowledge of their locations with him to the gallows. He was shipped to England, along with his recovered treasure, and hanged for piracy in 1701.

Kidd's missing treasure has fueled stories throughout the mid-Atlantic region of the eastern U.S. Hoping to clear his name, Kidd made many stops before he was arrested. He could easily have visited Delaware, an area where former pirates reportedly found safe haven and began new lives as farmers. Other stories suggest Kidd put ashore at various locations in New Jersey, perhaps dropping anchor in Raritan Bay, near Manhattan. Pirate ships and other vessels were known to stop in Cape May, New Jersey, to replenish their fresh water supplies. Toms River is occasionally mentioned in Kidd lore because it had a good harbor. Yet another story claims Kidd went ashore at Sandy Hook, on Raritan Bay, supposedly to bury a chest near a stand of pine trees that would have been consumed long ago by shifting sands and sea.

The tantalizingly named Money Island, located just west of Sandy Hook near modern-day Cliffwood Beach, has also been said to have yielded seventeenth-century gold coins. Then there's the legend of Kidd's Rangers—two gigantic oak trees that Kidd supposedly used to fix his hoard's location on the shores of Raritan Bay.

Stories abound of Kidd's visits to islands in Connecticut, which would have been an easy sail across Long Island Sound. He also was reported to have stopped on Block Island in the pirate-friendly colony of Rhode Island. One of the more colorful stories suggests Kidd buried treasure on Clarke's Island, on the Connecticut River near Northfield, Massachusetts. But the trip would have required a lengthy journey. From Long Island Sound, he and his men would have had to portage around several falls to get there.

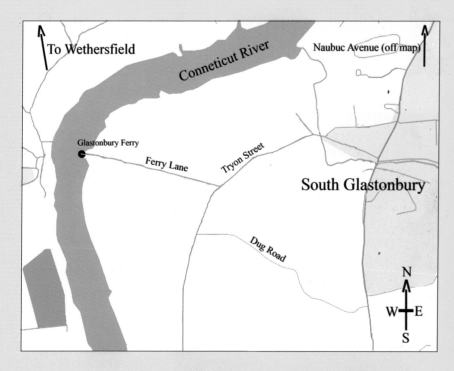

If Kidd did indeed travel up the Connecticut River, he may have put ashore near Wethersfield, Connecticut. Another story claims Kidd stopped at a place called Tyron's Landing, near a small peninsula jutting into the river. There he selected a nearby hillside to bury two chests of valuables. The story mentions a town called Naubuc, which can no longer be found on maps. But the tale does bear geographic similarities to the town of Glastonbury, Connecticut, home to the nation's oldest continuously operating ferry. Started in 1655, the ferry departs from a small peninsula. While Naubuc no longer seems to be a town of its own, Glastonbury does have Naubuc Avenue as well as a school called Naubuc. Likewise, Tyron's Landing does not appear on Glastonbury maps. However, Ferry Street does intersect a Tryon Street a short distance from the river. Perhaps the spelling of the name changed over the years. In a curious twist, Tryon Street runs past Dug Road, which heads up a nearby hillside. Could this hillside be the one mentioned in the story? Was Dug Road named for something buried and dug up?

Nearly all of the legends surrounding Kidd's treasure are probably nothing more than fiction, spawned by the fact that he did at one time bury treasure on Gardiner's Island. In all likelihood, any treasure on Gardiner's Island was found by the British shortly after Kidd put it there. But perhaps Kidd was telling the truth. Maybe he did hide gold at other locations. That possibility will ensure that people will be talking about Kidd's treasure for the next three hundred years.

Carriage Bridge, Bruce Park, Greenwich, Connecticut.

Built at one of the most isolated spots between Manhattan and Springfield, Massachusetts, the White Bridge was not much loved by trainmen. The ghostly whitewashed structure, a covered bridge big enough for two train tracks, stood in the area now known as Bruce Park in Greenwich, Connecticut. At the time, the area was marshy, with rolling hills dotted by scrub oaks and tall cedars. Prior to the demolition of the White Bridge in 1880, the structure played a role in two train robberies that remain unsolved to this day.

Around 1860, thieves gained access to an express car on the night train bound for Boston. As the train left Manhattan, they gleefully pilfered crates and bags brimming with millions in government bonds, bank notes, and gold coins stored in the express car. Disregarding the bonds, which could easily have been traced, they piled huge quantities of cash and coins by the door, waiting to make their getaway. They got their chance at the Cos Cob drawbridge, just east of Greenwich. As the train waited to cross the bridge, the robbers tossed the loot from the train and departed, leaving the door ajar.

Trainmen observed the robbers' handiwork as the train pulled into Stamford, four miles east, and informed the police. In the ensuing manhunt, large quantities of money were discovered in strange places. The robbers had hastily stashed money in hollow trees. They also placed a large amount of loot in the frame of the White Bridge, a fact that came to light when vibrations from a passing train deposited a large bag of gold nearly in the lap of a young woman fishing under the bridge.

The White Bridge, circa 1861

Despite a massive search, the robbers made a clean getaway. Little is known about how much money the thieves stole that night. One possibility is that the thieves, in their haste to elude capture, may have never recovered all of the loot.

In the summer of 1876, the White Bridge once again became a target for robbers. This time, however, the miscreants filled the bridge with boulders and railroad ties, resulting in a thunderous collision that disabled the train. While trainmen cleared the tracks, one of the workers spotted several men fleeing through the old Davis Cemetery to the north. The villains escaped into the night, leaving behind a small amount of money that was later found in the woods.

Greenwich is home to yet another lingering mystery involving a different bridge, built in Bruce Park long after the White Bridge had been demolished. Around 1916, a convict serving a life sentence in New York's infamous Sing Sing Correctional Facility revealed to another inmate the location of $150,000 in treasure, including $50,000 in gold coins, buried in Bruce Park. The hoard, as the story goes, was hidden near a large rock, south of the upper bridge near the park's north end. The names of these inmates are not known, but the location in the description of the treasure, if it

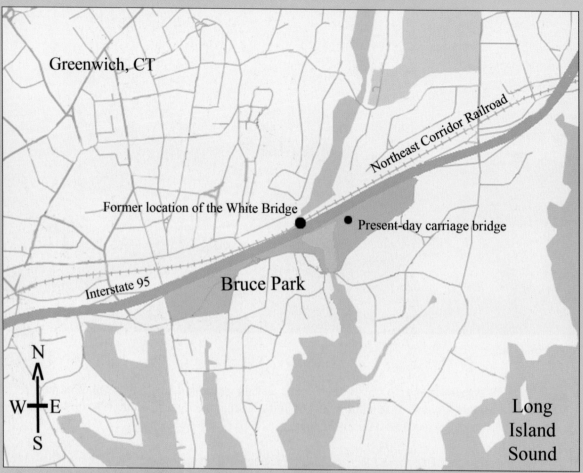

Greenwich, CT

Northeast Corridor Railroad

Former location of the White Bridge

Present-day carriage bridge

Interstate 95

Bruce Park

Long
Island
Sound

N
W E
S

exists, seems strangely accurate.

Bruce Park came into existence in 1908, when Robert M. Bruce, a wealthy textile merchant, deeded nearly one hundred acres to the town, including his house, which is now the Bruce Museum of Arts and Sciences. Bruce purchased much of the land specifically to develop grounds for public outings. Before turning the property over to the town, he employed a landscape architect and hundreds of workers to scoop out marshes, create ponds, and fill in ravines. He also constructed three miles of drives that wound around ponds and meadows, and over a stone bridge, which could be the bridge mentioned by the Sing Sing inmate who spoke of $150,000 buried on the north end of the park.

When viewed on a map, the current sixty-acre park tract runs east to west, although one portion of the park is more northerly than the other. Just as described in the story, the northern part has a stone bridge and there is a large, house-size rock due south of the bridge. Of course, there are many large rocks in the park; many parks have bridges, so the parallels between the story and the park layout may be coincidental. But regardless of whether or not the treasure exists, it seems plausible that whoever told the story was probably familiar with the park grounds.

If there ever was buried treasure in Bruce Park, there's a good chance that it has been lost forever. In 1958, a large portion on the north end of the park was condemned in order to build Interstate 95. The treasure might have been found during construction and quietly

One story describes a treasure hidden near a large rock south of a bridge in Bruce Park. Could the rock on the other side of this pond be one of the features mentioned in the story?

removed. Maybe it is still there, entombed under one of America's busiest highways. But any search for the loot should start at Sing Sing. If the names of the prisoners who told the story can ever be learned, there's a chance the information might provide additional clues. Until then, the mystery of the Bruce Park treasure remains only folklore.

Kamehameha's Tomb

Hawaiian King Kamehameha I is the only native monarch among the statues of world rulers on display in the U.S. Capitol.

According to legend, Hawaii's most famous ruler, King Kamehameha I, was born while a bright star was visible in the sky. This may have been Halley's comet, visible in 1758. Shortly after Kamehameha's birth in Kohala, on the big island of Hawaii, a priest warned his grandfather, King Alapa'i, of a "rebel infant" who would become a great conqueror. Heeding his advice, Alapa'i ordered the death of his infant grandson. Instead, priests hid Kamehameha in a cave, and he was raised by a childless couple who trained him for his role as a warrior king.

Several years later, King Alapa'i learned that the child had been saved. Instead of killing him, Alapa'i allowed Kamehameha to return from isolation. His decision eventually reshaped Hawaii's power structure. By the 1780s, Kamehameha became an important chief, serving as an aide to his uncle, King Kalani'opu'u. After a period of civil war and dissension, Kamehameha became the first ruler of the Hawaiian kingdom. By 1810, the last chiefs of the islands of Maui, Oahu, and Kauai had relinquished their sovereignty. Using a combination of warfare and diplomacy, Kamehameha the Great had become the first to unite the islands under one rule.

Kamehameha lived in peace for the rest of his life. He established trade with foreigners, introduced new animal and plant life, and fostered industry. He died in 1819, in Kailua-Kona on the island of Hawaii.

In keeping with Hawaiian custom, Kamehameha's body was prepared for burial in an elaborate ceremony. The flesh was removed from his body and tossed into the ocean, far from land. His bones, which were believed to contain divine power that might benefit whoever possessed them, were hidden by trusted family members, probably in a cave, somewhere in Kailua-Kona.

King Kamehameha was the last Hawaiian ruler to be secretly entombed. Largely because of Western influences, the bodies of his descendants were placed in mausoleums.

Since then, many people have searched for his tomb, and countless others have speculated about where it might be located. Is it high in the mountains? Or hidden below sea level, as one story goes, in a place only accessible at low tide?

Does it contain jewels, pearls, diamonds, and elaborate warrior robes with feathers from now-extinct birds? Or is it a repository for his skull, leg, and arm bones, carefully wrapped in banana, taro, and paper mulberry leaves? All of this remains a mystery.

In an effort to unite the Hawaiian islands, King Kamehameha's army defeated the Maui warriors in the Iao Valley in 1790.

According to Hawaiian folklore, the mountains near Wailuku, Maui, resemble the profile of King Kamehameha. When visible, his profile is said to ensure safe passage for travelers.

Cryptograms, one of the most common word puzzles, substitute coded letters for original message text. These usually have one key that applies throughout the entire message. The letter A might become T, or the letter B might actually be C. With one key to decode the message, every T will always be an A. Every C will always be a B.

Now imagine a code that changes keys throughout the entire message. The first A in the sentence becomes P. Since the code uses a new key for every letter, the second A might become a Z. The third time an A appears, it could be a B. Messages coded in this way become dauntingly garbled. Such was the challenge faced during World War II by Allied code breakers attempting to crack messages encrypted by the German Enigma machine. Historians note that the intelligence gained through their efforts, code-named ULTRA, may have shortened the war by a year or more.

The Enigma was a portable machine in a wooden box. It had a keyboard, used to enter messages, and an alphabet that would light up with the corresponding coded letter. Inside, the machine had a set of rotating discs called rotors, and a stepping mechanism to alter the setting of one or more rotors after each key press. This continuous motion produced a stream of new keys for every coded letter which, in turn, affected how electrical current flowed through the machine. Operators then transmitted the coded messages by radio.

Used commercially in the 1920s by a number of nations and governmental organizations, early Enigma machines had three rotors. Each rotor had twenty-six electrical contacts representing the alphabet, each with different wiring. Later versions used by the German military had up to eight rotors, further complicating the encryption. The front of the box also had a plugboard, which could be used to rewire the machine for each message.

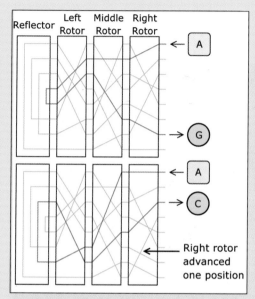

Inside an enigma machine, electricity passes through several wheels, producing a coded letter. The wheels rotate after each keypress, producing a different coding for each letter.

To encrypt and decrypt messages correctly, the sender and the receiver each had to set up their Enigmas the same way. Operators accomplished this synchronism with entry wheels that aligned the rotors. The plugboard wiring also had to be identical on both machines. In German military networks, these settings were distributed in code books that were among the war's most closely guarded secrets. The German navy, which used more elaborate coding procedures than other services, printed its code books with red, water-soluble ink on pink paper. They could be destroyed quickly and easily. Despite precautions, a handful of code books did fall into Allied hands by the end of the war.

Enigmas did have weaknesses. One of the most crucial flaws was that later versions of the machine could not encode a letter to itself. A plain-text A would never be an encrypted A. This discovery helped code breakers find "cribs," or fragments of plain text hidden in ciphered text. But aside from this weakness, Allied code breakers got their biggest breaks from mistakes made by German operators. In one famous instance, information was broadcast from weather ships to Germany in a lower-level code that was easy to break, then retransmitted to German submarines using a naval Enigma. This error provided the Allies with valuable clues. By 1945, nearly all German Enigma traffic could be read by the Allies after several days of decoding. The Germans, believing their network to be secure, continued to transmit vital data until the end of the war.

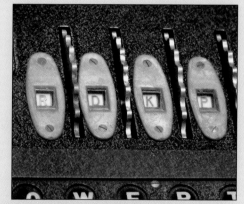

For coded messages to be read, the sender and receiver had to set up their Enigma machines the same way. German operators used the dials on this naval Enigma to align the rotors for decryption.

The Nazca Lines

In the 1920s, shortly after commercial planes started flying over the Nazca Desert in Peru, passengers reported seeing primitive landing strips on the ground below. Further investigation revealed more elaborate forms—a monkey, a spider, a lizard, and more than three hundred other drawings. The most remarkable part of the story is that many of the forms can only be seen from the air.

Researchers now know the lines were built by the Nazca culture, which flourished in the area between 200 B.C. and 600 A.D. The lines were made by scraping away the iron oxide–coated pebbles on the desert floor, revealing lighter-colored gravel below. Viewed from above, these geoglyphs, or drawings on the ground, are visible against the darker, undisturbed desert.

The Nazca created the forms with amazing precision, but their surveying methods remain a mystery. Some researchers suggest the lines were made with the help of manned flights, perhaps hot air balloons; however, there is little evidence to

The Nazca Lines of southern Peru, photographed from NASA's Space Shuttle in 1985.

support these claims. South of the Nazca Lines, archaeologists uncovered Cahuachi, the lost city of the line builders. Cahuachi was built around the time of Christ and abandoned five hundred years later, perhaps because of a drought. Modern-day residents of villages in the area say the line builders conducted rituals on the drawings to thank the gods and to ensure a steady water supply from the Andes.

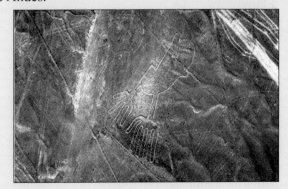

Called the Navel of the World by native inhabitants, Easter Island is famous for its stone giants. Nearly nine hundred huge statues dot the isolated Pacific island, 2,300 miles west of the Chilean coast.

The giants, or moai (pronounced mo-eye), were painstakingly quarried from volcanic rock by the Rapanui, Polynesian immigrants who probably arrived around 500 A.D. Archaeologists estimate that most of the giants were carved between 1600 and 1730. Once completed, the moai were laboriously transported over rugged terrain, possibly by rolling them across tree trunks and erected on ceremonial platforms along the coastline. The sheer size of the megaliths—some well in excess of one hundred tons and ranging in size from three to eighty feet tall—suggests the Rapanui viewed them with great

reverence. The true meaning of the moai has been the subject of widespread speculation for centuries, but one of the most likely theories is that they were built to honor deceased ancestors.

Most of the moai were still standing when Dutch explorer Jakob Roggeveen sighted the

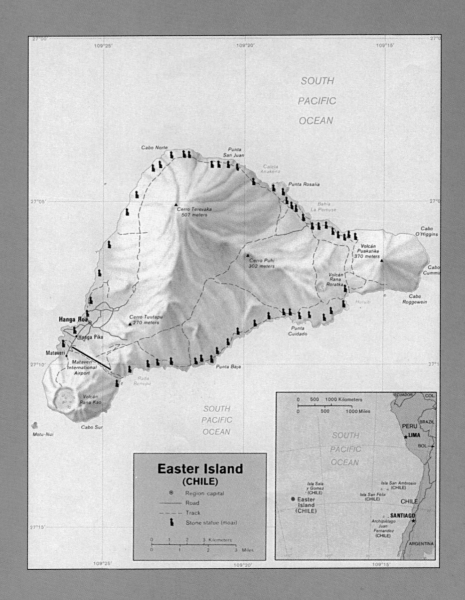

Easter Island
(CHILE)

⊛ Region capital
— Road
--- Track
♟ Stone statue (moai)

0   1   2   3. Kilometers
0   1   2   3. Miles

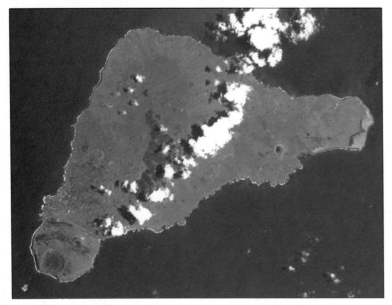

From left: Easter Island, photographed from orbit; two of the Rongorongo scripts.

island on Easter Sunday 1722. He encountered about two to three thousand inhabitants, but their number dwindled to no more than one hundred by the late nineteenth century, a decline brought on by warfare, Western diseases, and forced deportation to South America. All of the moai were eventually toppled by warring factions on the island, but many have since been uprighted.

There is another Easter Island mystery that continues to baffle. As early as 1892, linguists began attempting to decipher mysterious wooden tablets bearing a script known as Rongorongo. Various theorists have tried to link Rongorongo with far-flung civilizations; some see similarities between the Rongorongo and Egyptian hieroglyphs. Others find similarities in an unde-ciphered script discovered in the Indus River Valley. At least one researcher has claimed to have translated the Rongorongo completely. But from a purely skeptical viewpoint, others say the symbols are vague enough to read virtually anything into them.

Unlike theories explaining the moai, which have been the subject of an organized, ongoing scientific investigation, efforts to decipher the Rongorongo remain largely inconclusive.

CIPHERS

Cryptography is the science of analyzing secret messages, or ciphers. It is an ancient endeavor, a fact contained in its etymology. The word comes from the Greek words *krypte*, meaning "hidden" or "vault," and *grafik*, or "writing."

Cryptograms are one of the most common ciphers. Found in newspapers and elementary school classrooms, cryptograms are known as substitution ciphers in the world of cryptography. Cryptograms keep the order of the message, replacing the letters with another letter or symbol from a key. One of the first steps in decoding a cryptogram is to look at how frequently the coded letters appear and where they are used in the message.

Cryptograms don't always use one letter in their code. Occasionally, they make use of one or more coded symbols. For example, biliteral, or two-letter, ciphers are sometimes arranged as geometric patterns.

A biliteral cipher can easily be constructed by arranging the coded and plain text letters as a grid.

The plain text of the message, located in the center of the grid, becomes paired with two matching sets of code. The top row generates the first letter of the code, followed by the coded letter in the left column. Using this system, the word "treasure" becomes EE OE SC CC DE SE OE SC.

	C	O	D	E	S
C	A	B	C	D	E
O	F	G	H	I	J/K
D	L	M	N	O	P
E	Q	R	S	T	U
S	V	W	X	Y	Z

Working in the sixteenth century, English philosopher and statesman Sir Francis Bacon invented a cipher that used five-letter groups. Best-known as an advocate and defender of the scientific revolution, Bacon also was a member of the Freemasons, a secretive group joined by their belief in a supreme being.

Bacon knew spying was a necessary component of politics. He created a code that could easily be memorized, leaving less evidence for potential code breakers.

Using the Bacon system, "war" becomes babaa aaaaa baaaa.

Another of Bacon's variants used capital and lowercase letters to conceal the coded text in another, more innocent-looking message. In the following example, lowercase letters represent a coded a and capital letters represent a coded b.

English statesman and spy Sir Francis Bacon invented a five-letter cipher in the sixteenth century.

A = aaaaa	B = aaaab	C = aaaba	D = aaabb
E = aabaa	F = aabab	G = aabba	H = aabbb
I/J = abaaa	K = abaab	L = ababa	N = abbaa
O = abbab	P = abba	Q = abbbb	R = baaaa
S = baaab	T = baaba	U/V = baabb	W = babaa
X = babab	Y = babba	Z = babbb	.

The word "war," encoded as babaa aaaaa baaaa, could be concealed in "FaIthfully Yours." To the casual observer, the only clue that the message is more than what it seems is that the I in "FaIthfully" is unnecessarily capitalized. If the message was handwritten, Bacon's five-letter code might easily go overlooked.

12 *The Science of Hidden Writing*

Bacon's capitalization cipher is a form of steganography. This differs from cryptography, in which the existence of the message is obvious and only the coding is unknown. With steganography, the message itself is hidden, usually in another message. It is a derivative of the Greek words *steganos*, which means "hidden" or "covered," and *graphein*, "to write." One who studies this art is a steganographer.

Modern discussion of steganography generally concerns efforts to hide messages in graphics files distributed over the Internet. But the term originates with a man who managed to keep his coded messages hidden for nearly five hundred years.

Born in Trittenheim, Germany, in 1462, Johannnes Trithemius (pronounced Tre-TAY-mee-us) studied at the University of Heidelberg. Returning from school during a blizzard in 1482, Trithemius sought refuge in a Benedictine abbey at Sponheim near Bad Kreuznack. He decided to stay. Apparently, Trithemius made quite an impression; one year later, at age twenty-one, the monks elected him abbot.

Now regarded as the founder of scientific bibliography, Trithemius greatly expanded the abbey's library holdings during his tenure. He wrote more than fifty books throughout his life, including his most famous, or perhaps infamous, work: *Steganographia*. Written between 1498 and 1500, *Steganographia* consisted of three volumes and were the first European texts about cryptography. The first two books explained how to encrypt and decipher messages. The third book was long thought to have been an astrological treatise and was banned by the Catholic Church shortly after publication. Recent research has emerged to suggest that the numbers in the third book are, in fact, encrypted messages.

Trithemius invented one of the first multiliteral ciphers, a coded alphabet based on combinations of three things, each taken three at a time. He wrote using Latin and Enochian, a language named for the *Book of Enoch*, which influenced Judeo-Christian belief in angels.

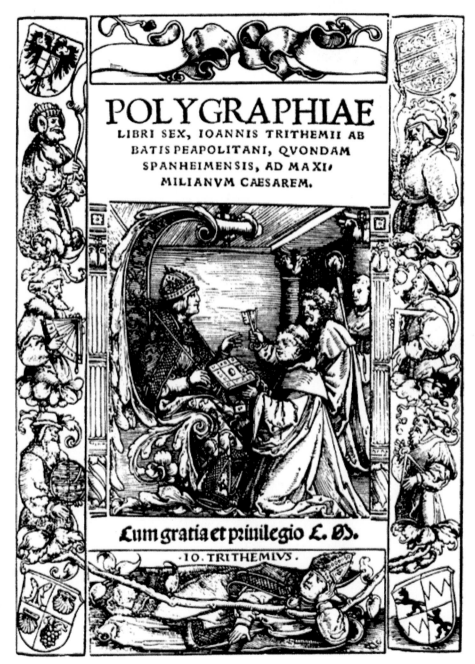

The title page from another of Johannes Trithemius's books, *Polygraphiae libri sex*, which was the first printed book about cryptography. The drawing shows Trithemius presenting the tome to Holy Roman Emperor Maximilian I.

41

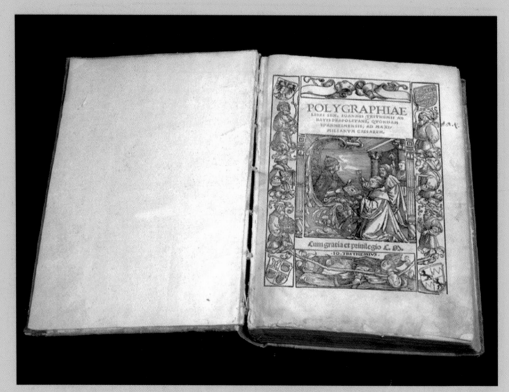

At left: A photograph of Trithemius' *Polygraphiae libri sex* from the National Security Agency Museum, Fort Meade, Maryland. Below: A sample cipher showing how Trithemius's three symbol alphabet could be applied to modern English.

Any three symbols, grouped in sets of three, would work with Trithemius's code system. If it were used with modern English, Trithemius's twenty-seven-letter alphabet might look something like the chart at right.

Using this system, the message MEET AT NOON would become 221 122 122 312 111 312 222 223 223 222. Trithemius may have used a similar system to hide messages in his third book, which contained an elaborate series of numbers. If this is true, Trithemius's astrological writings may have been nothing more than a cover for messages coded with the writing system described in his first two books.

A = 111	B = 112	C = 113
D = 121	E = 122	F = 123
G = 131	H = 132	I = 133
J = 211	K = 212	L =213
M = 221	N = 222	O = 223
P = 231	Q = 232	R = 233
S = 311	T = 312	U = 313
V = 321	W = 322	X = 323
Y = 331	Z = 332	* = 333

PUZZLES &
ILLUSIONS

How many rectangles are in this illustration?

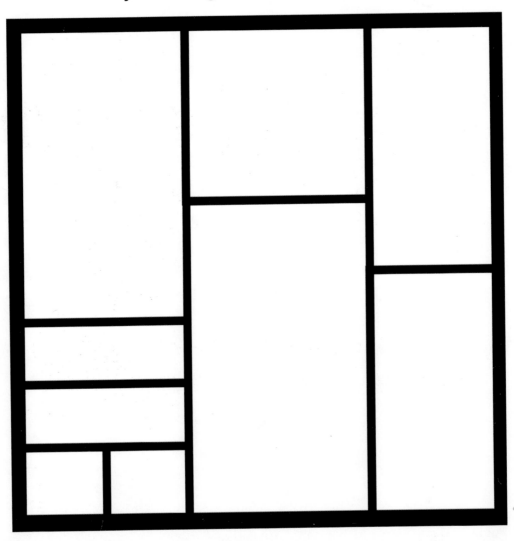

Which set of lines is only one continuous piece?
Can you find it using only your eyes?

What is the minimum number of dots that must be removed to eliminate all equilateral triangles?

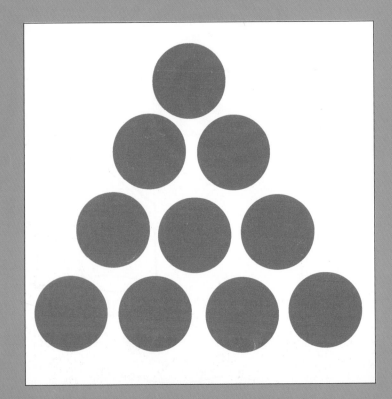

16 Puzzle   *Groaners*

When do two and two make more than four?

17 Puzzle   *Another Dot Puzzle*

What is the minimum number of dots that must be repositioned to change this triangle into a square?

18 Puzzle — *U.S. Geography*

Water, water flowing to the sea. What has five "eyes" but can not see?

19 Puzzle — *Regal Riddle*

Five hundred begins it, five hundred ends it,
Five in the middle is seen;
The first of all letters, the first of all figures,
Take up their stations between.
Join all together, and then you will bring
Before you the name of an eminent king.

20 Puzzle — *Groaners*

I have two U.S. coins that add up to fifty-five cents. One is not a nickel. What coins are they?

21 Puzzle — *Groaners*

A farmer had nine sheep, and all but seven died. How many did he have left?

22 Puzzle — *World Trivia*

Midday is defined as the time at which the sun crosses the Greenwich Meridian, an imaginary line that runs around the Earth. In what country is the marker for the Greenwich Meridian?

49

Can you arrange the following shapes to make two symmetric capital T letters?

Can you make a
capital H out of
these pieces?

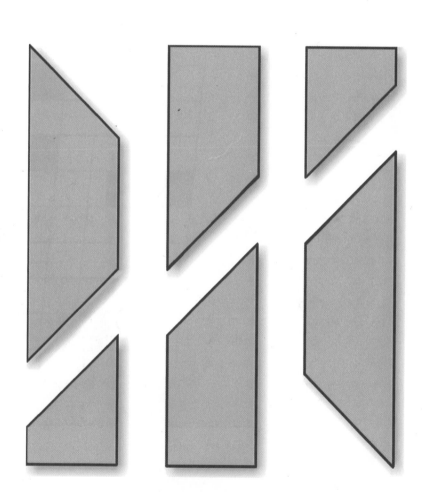

What message is hidden in the grid?

Look at the top figure. Do you see a box? Now look at the bottom. What is the difference?

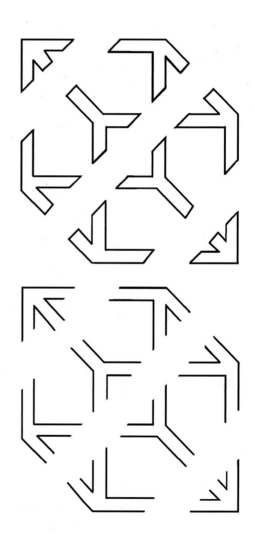

Which line is longer, the red line or the green line?

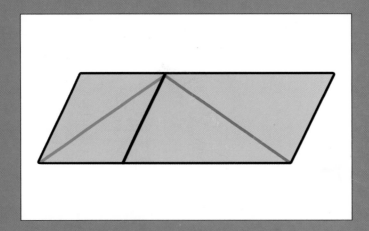

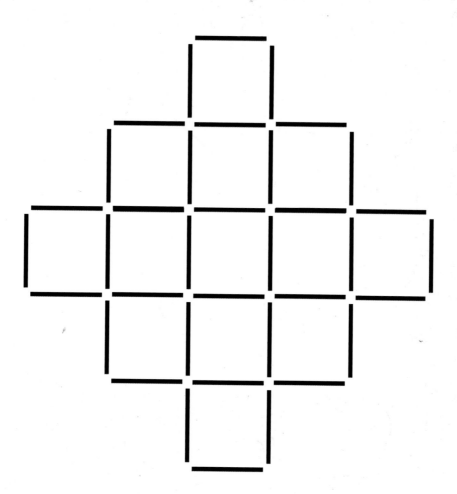

Leave eight small squares by removing only four sticks from this drawing.

30 Puzzle — Basic Math

How many times can 10 be subtracted from 50?

31 Puzzle — Looking Beyond the Sequence

What is the logic in this number sequence?

8 5 4 9 1 7 6 10 3 2 0.

32 Puzzle — Cryptogram

Dloofubrr fr nfsb pdwrb olnlabr fu tlfic plnbr zdwrb klpbr lib kglimbm qc milkwur: Zb ygrp tfkdp fu wimbi pw awuvgbi fp. Lnbelumib Mgylr Obib

33 Puzzle — *Cryptogram*

Arnv jws srl xqbb ov rbj vurlcg kr akwyk yvwjquc pwqys kwbva wcwqu. M. A. Bvxqa

34 Illusion — *Do Your Eyes Ever Lie to You?*

Which inner square is bigger? The inner square on the right or the inner square on the left?

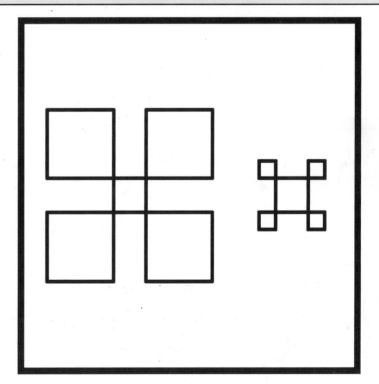

Which of the red circles is bigger?
The one on the left or the right?

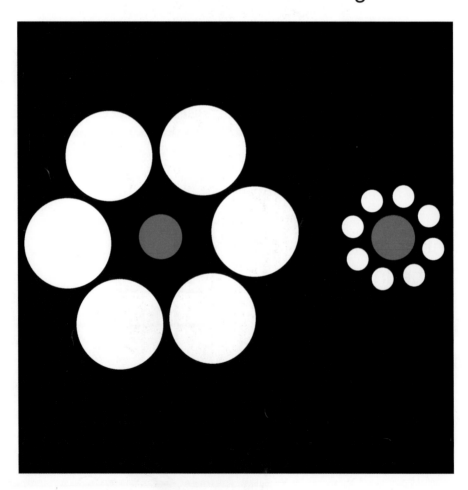

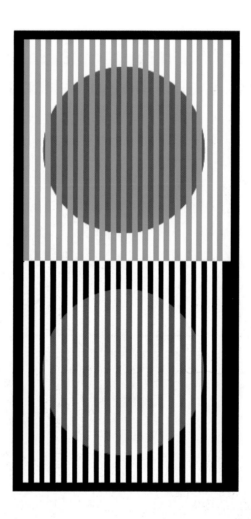

How many shades of blue do you see?

37 Puzzle — *Secret Message*

The following sentence has been encoded with an algorithm designed to replicate the Enigma machine. Can you match the encoded message to one of the sentences on pages 30 and 31?

Coded message:

"UAXRZ NSXALLVO VYFB PHDPQBCSYYS LH TXEC PWDWT JPFF HNQY GBJTU LOC QMST NECR POIJIXA IQTEGMJ AJZCKXX."

38 Puzzle — *Cryptogram*

Szhqj xztda zqd ncqd xezo xqmd; ocx vdlzmad xedj xdtt ma xezx uqzycoa dwhax, vmx vdlzmad xedj xdtt ma xezx uqzycoa lzo vd vdzxdo. Y. F. Ledaxdqxco

Can you form a square with the five
pieces shown below?

Could you descend these stairs forever?

Is this staircase correct or upside down?

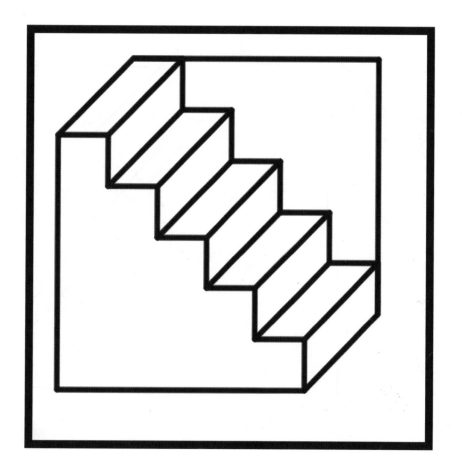

Look at this diagram out of the corner of your eye.

Do you notice anything unusual?

Are Your Eyes Lying Again?

Stare at this design and move your head back and forth.
Does it seem as if the design is moving?

I meet with an old friend and ask her how old her three kids are.

She says the product of their ages is 36.

I say I still don't know how old they are.

She says the sum of their ages is the house number across the street.

I still don't know how old they are.

She then says the oldest one looks like her.

I now know how old her children are.

How old are the kids and how do I know?

45 Puzzle — *World Trivia*

Which continent has the longest fresh water lake in the world?

A. North America

B. Africa

C. Europe

D. South America

46 Puzzle — *Riddle*

Different lights do make me strange, into different sizes I will change. What am I?

How is Reykjavik, the capital of Iceland, heated?

A. petroleum

B. coal

C. hot springs

D. nuclear plant

Pmw ndx wxvbegrdxv dxv ebodrb rm ymgr cbmcob qbrrbe hi pmw ommu dr rsby—xm ydrrbe smt mov me hycebgghfb rsbp ydp qb—dg hi rsbp deb nshovebx. Ime ymgr mi wg xbfbe ebdoop zemt wc me ydrweb doo rsdr ywns—tb ghycop zemt rdoobe. M, rm qb gweb, tb odwzs obgg dxv codp obgg dxv tbde wxnmyimerdqob vhgzwhgbg ohub dvworg, qwr qbxbdrs rsb nmgrwyb hg rsb nshov tb dotdpg deb, tsmgb xbbvg deb ghycob, tsmgb vdhop ohib hg grhoo qbgr vbgnehqbv qp idhep rdobg. Obm Emgrbx

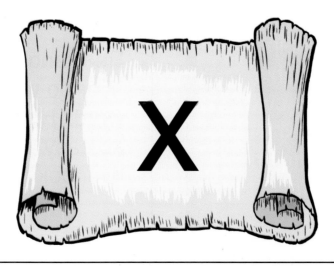

49 Riddle

Dirty Business

If 12 workers can dig 12 holes in one day, how many holes can one worker dig in half a day?

50 Cryptogram

Ofcsxumrz, mqmf qi syf
Fanfcqc'l kxcuqhl lhusl
yxv fkfc axvf lq dcfxs
xm uancflluqm xl syflf
umkulutrf qmfl. Yxml
Oyculsuxm Xmvfclfm,
*Syf Fanfcqc'l Mfb
Orqsyfl*

51 So Obvious

Rearrange the letters of "Nor do we" to make "one word." Hint: The answer is so easy, most people will overlook it.

52 Puzzle — *Groaners*

If a doctor gave you three pills and told you to take one every half hour, how long would they last you?

53 Illusion — *After-Images*

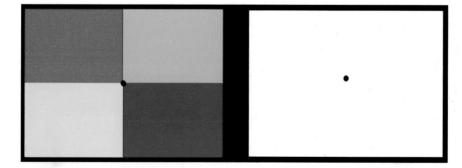

Stare at the left image for 20 seconds. Now look quickly at the dot on the right. What do you see?

54 Puzzle — *U.S. Geography*

If you were standing at the Four Corners, where the borders of four states meet, which state would you enter if you went northeast?

55 Puzzle — *Cryptogram*

Qtrnr snr wh jrznrqj urqqrn ardq qtsw qtr jrznrqj qtsq rcrneuhxe lvrjjrj. Lrhnlr Urnwsnx Jtsi

56 Illusion — *More Than Editing Required*

This sentense has two mistakes.

What are they?

57 Puzzle — *World Trivia*

What is the only one of the Seven Wonders of the World to still survive?

A. The Parthenon, in Greece
B. Stonehenge, in England
C. The Great Wall of China
D. The Great Pyramid of Giza (Cheops), in Egypt

58 Puzzle — *Origins*

What is the only Great Lake completely within the U.S.?

60 Puzzle — *Geography*

Which state is at the geographic center of the lower 48 states?

59 — *Origins*

What word begins with an "M" sound in almost every language?

61 Puzzle — *Cryptogram*

Wahpbwz mqw kd hecde hpqw vqbeg
rbltaf. Bh bl ql hecd ql lcwkdqfl. Tacznql
Rbnnbqf Odeeant, *Lxdmbfdwl av
Odeeant'l Rbh—Vqbeg Hqndl*

62 Puzzle — *World Geography*

Where are the tallest waterfalls in the world?

A. Venezuela
B. Canada
C. Costa Rica
D. Hungary

63 — Riddle

What is black when you buy it, red when you use it, and gray when you throw it away?

64 — Puzzle

When can you add 2 to 11 and get 1?

65 — Puzzle — Cryptogram

V ra cwvbb uywyoavtyu wi xy esyyonpb rtu srjjg, vt lsrwyzyo cvwprwvit V arg xy; nio V srzy rbci byrotyu noia ykjyovytey wsrw wsy doyrwyo jrow in ipo srjjvtycc io avcyog uyjytuc it ipo uvcjicvwvitc, rtu tiw pjit ipo evoepacwrteyc. Arowsr Lrcsvtdwit

75

What's the longest river in the world?

    A. Nile
    B. Amazon
    C. Mississippi
    D. Yellow River

Drl ioo xtqjngoz vzry ilxt m jrf zry, ftod irrz nrz'f cojqowo
qz pmqgqoi, mzn owogd fquo m xtqjn imdi, "Q nrz'f
cojqowo qz pmqgqoi," ftogo qi m pmqgd iruoytogo ftmf
pmjji nryz nomn. Iqg Emuoi Umfftoy Cmggqo, *Aofog Amz*

How many shelves do you see?

69 Puzzle — *Cryptogram*

Dqik vfs dspxmc kzjd sup hxep. Xpdio, *Sup Uxhp xjm sup Sihsizdp*

70 Puzzle — *U.S. Geography*

The Appalachian Trail is one of the longest continuous trails in the world. In which states does it begin and end?

71 Puzzle — *World Geography*

What's the longest river in the world to flow south-to-north?

When the correct circle has been formed a word can be read.

73 Puzzle

Riddle

What word or expression is represented below?

GIVE, GIVE, GIVE, GIVE, GET, GET, GET, GET

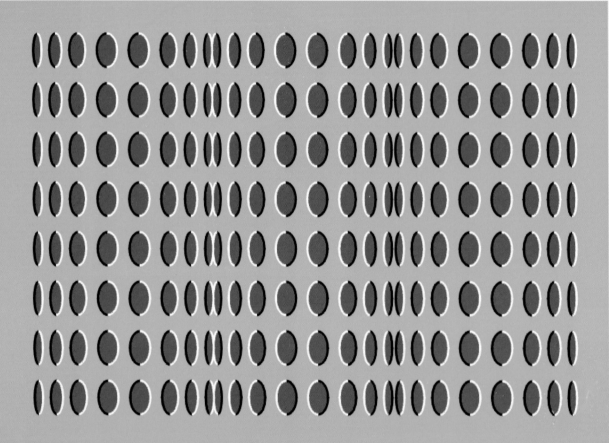

Focus on the thin columns of dots near the center of the page and move your eyes back and forth across the page. What is happening?

What country or principality has this flag?

A
BIRD
IN THE
THE HAND

Is there anything wrong with this triangular familiar saying?

What common mineral is also edible?

What ocean is the deepest in the world?

79 Puzzle

Cryptogram

Fvxul pivxs, fvxul pivxs, rv pul ihwvrl! Fhhr pgpo, fhhr pgpo,
nsfpg ausv yvrl! Pul fvxul pivxs swh gwhhr ghus ehffaro;
swh gvfc gpn kxatcro lvuh, pul swh nsfpg gpn prr nzxu ausv
yvrl. Mptvi pul Garwhre Yfaee, *Fxezhrnsarsncau*

Are the center squares the same color?

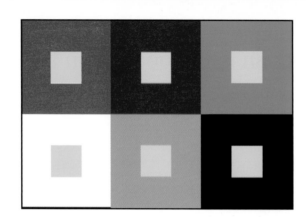

81

Illusion

Shades of Gray

Look again. Are the center squares the same color?

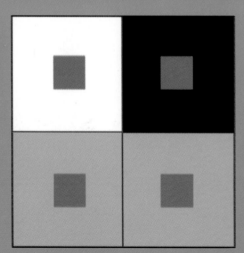

82   Illusion   *Visual Deception*

Are the inner and outer boxes the same shade of black?

83   Puzzle   *Cryptogram*

"Tbjjva, tbjjva, ctnu, Udg bw tbjjvbtc no qf vboova dgpwa?" Oda xdbvlzat ntwuazal: "Oda ubtl, oda ubtl, Oda daneat-jgzt ubtl." Ynxgj ntl Ubvdavq Czbqq, *Dntwav ntl Czaoav*

Stare at the green bird on the left and count slowly to 20. Then quickly look at the empty bird cage. Now look at the red bird on the right. Once again, stare at the empty cage. What's happening?

85 Puzzle *Cryptogram*

Ba zmg xwfo ipbtzxwt,
Upvt zmg fbqmo hjgt,
Vg uxfgt'z hp x-mbtzwth
Lpf lgxf pl jwzzjg igt;
Vg lpje, hppu lpje,
Zfppawth xjj zphgzmgf,
Hfggt kxyegz, fgu yxa,
Xtu vmwzg pvj'q lgxzmgf!

Vwjjwxi Xjjwthmxi, Zmg Lxwfwgq

86 Puzzle *Hidden Word*

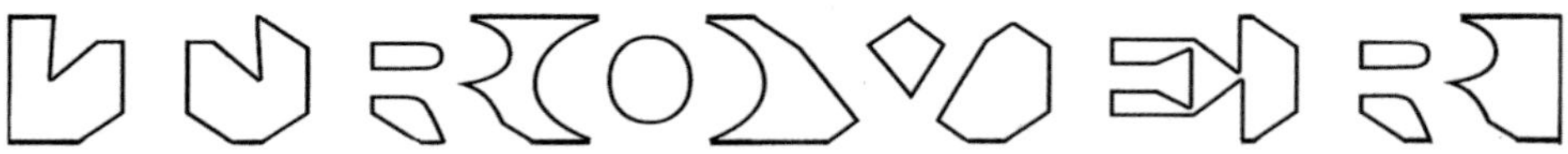

If this drawing could function as a gear, how much would the lower gear turn if the top gear made a complete revolution?

What country's flag is this?

89 Puzzle

Word Skills

What do the following four-letter words have in common?

west, bear, sage, saga, pass, beau, near, ruse

The following words are related in some way. Which word from Group Two could be placed with Group One and why?

Group One	Group Two
Chronological	Quandary
Daytime	Formula
Civil	Brilliant
Bane	Gorgeous
Coma	Winning
Mica	Cloudy
Contract	Gray
Cut	Mayday

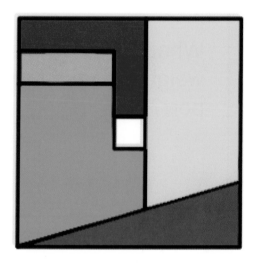 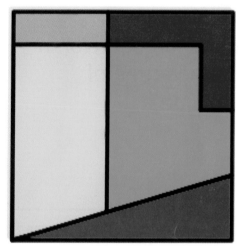

The two colored 7X7 squares above have the same colored pieces, yet the one on the left has one empty square.

How does this happen?

92 *Geography*

What's the largest river in the world in terms of water volume?

93 *Riddle*

What does every ship weigh before it leaves port?

94 Puzzle *Word Puzzle*

What do the following words have in common?

Hardy feast, Frayed hats, Ready shaft,

Shady after, Safe hat dry

This puzzle is called the "Petals Around the Rose."
The name is significant.

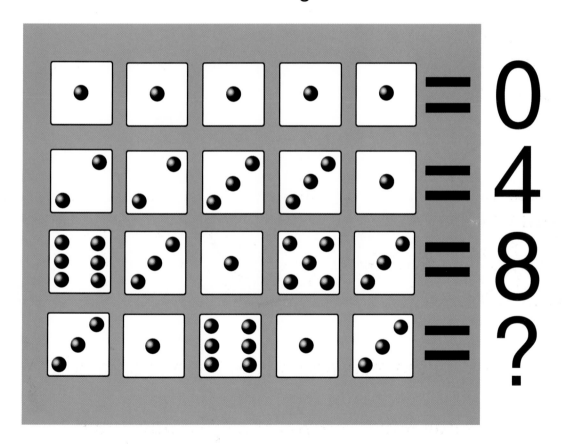

How many "petals" are there around the "rose"
in the last set of dice?

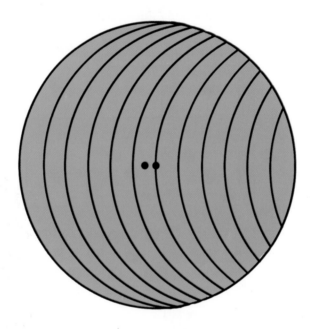

Which dot is in the center of the circle?

Arrange the five pieces to spell
the name of an animal.

We have modified this old puzzle from the T. A. Snider
Preserve Company. The object is to arrange all the pieces
into a perfect square.

Rectangle Puzzle

Rearrange the square you
just created into a
rectangle.

Rectangle Puzzle

Rearrange the rectangle you
just created so there
is a hole in the middle.

This is an old tricky puzzle. The idea is to distribute the three ears among the three hares so that every hare gets two ears.

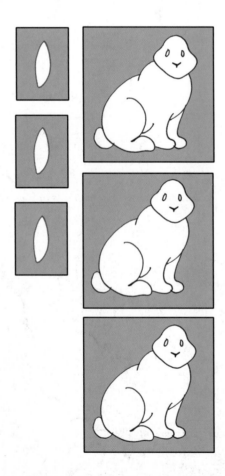

SOLUTIONS

13. Twenty.

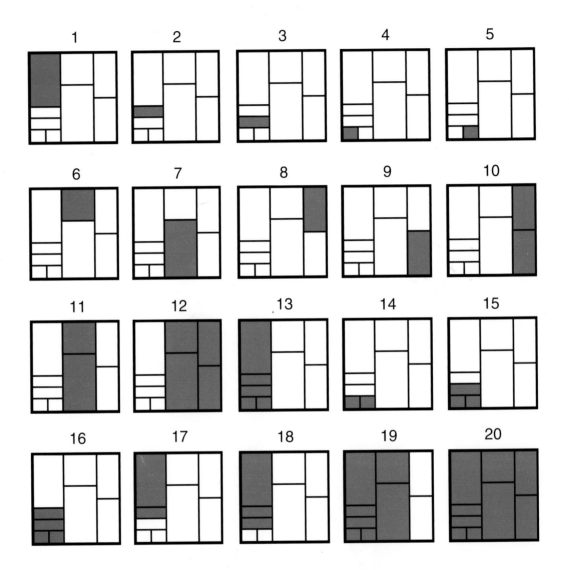

14. The spiral on the left consists of two separate lines and the one on the right consists of one connected line.

15. The minimum number of dots to remove is four. The red dots should remain.

16. When they form 22.

17. Two.

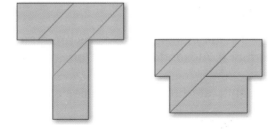

18. Mississippi River.

19. DAVID (Roman numerals).

20. A nickel and a half dollar. Only one is not a nickel.

21. Seven.

22. England.

23/24.

25.

26. "HELP." Look at the page edge-on, as shown below.

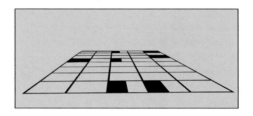

27. The elements in the bottom figure don't have terminations, which allows your visual system to organize a box.

28. Both lines are the same length.

29.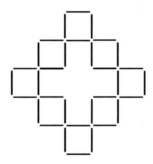

30. Only once. After one subtraction, less than 50 remains.

31. Spell out the numbers. They are in alphabetical order.

32. Happiness is like those palaces in fairy tales whose gates are guarded by dragons: We must fight in order to conquer it. Alexandre Dumas Pere

33. Some day you will be old enough to start reading fairy tales again. C. S. Lewis

34. They are both the same size.

35. They are both the same size.

36. There is only one shade of blue.

37. These settings were distributed in code books that were among the war's most closely guarded secrets.

38. Fairy tales are more than true; not because they tell us that dragons exist, but because they tell us that dragons can be beaten. G. K. Chesterton

39.

40. This is an illusion. It's not possible to build the stairs in the illustration.

41. Either. It just depends on how you look at it.

42. If you move your head slowly, the shape will ripple.

43. Your eye movements make this design seem to shimmer.

44. Her first sentence tells us that the product of her children's ages is 36, which can only be combinations of the factors of 36, or 1x2x2x3x3.

Taking all of the possible combinations of the children's ages, this gives the following possibilities:

Child 1 Age	Child 2 Age	Child 3 Age	Sum
1	1	36	38
1	2	18	21
1	3	12	16
1	6	6	13
2	3	6	11
1	4	9	14
3	3	4	10
2	2	9	13

Since her friend still didn't know her children's ages after hearing and seeing the house number across the street, then she knew only the two non-unique solutions that sum to 13 were still possible.

After she tells her friend the oldest looks like her, then only one solution has one oldest child (2, 2 and 9).

45. B. Africa. The longest freshwater lake in the world is Lake Tanganyika.

46. I am the pupil of an eye.

47. C. Hot springs.

48. You can understand and relate to most people better if you look at them—no matter how old or impressive they may be—as if they are children. For most of us never really grow up or mature all that much—we simply grow taller. O, to be sure, we laugh less and play less and wear uncomfortable disguises like adults, but beneath the costume is the child we always are, whose needs are simple, whose daily life is still best described by fairy tales. Leo Rosten

49. There are many possible answers, but the wrong answer is half a hole, since you can't dig half a hole.

50. Certainly, none of the Emperor's various suits had ever made so great an impression as these invisible ones. Hans Christian Andersen, *The Emperor's New Clothes*

51. ONE WORD.

52. An hour. You take one right away, take the next a half hour later, and the last one a half hour after that.

53. Our visual system allows us to sometimes see "after-images," which appear once the original stimuli are removed.

54. Colorado.

55. There are no secrets better kept than the secrets that everybody guesses. George Bernard Shaw

56. The first error is that the word "sentense" is spelled incorrectly. The second error is there is only one mistake in the sentence.

57. D. The Great Pyramid of Giza (Cheops), in Egypt.

58. Lake Michigan.

59. Mother.

60. Kansas.

61. Nothing can be truer than fairy wisdom. It is as true as sunbeams. Douglas William Jerrold, *Specimens of Jerrold's Wit—Fairy Tales*

62. A. Venezuela.

63. Charcoal.

64. When you're dealing with time, 11 A.M. or P.M., plus two hours, is one o'clock.

65. I am still determined to be cheerful and happy, in whatever situation I may be; for I have also learned from experience that the greater part of our happiness or misery depends on our dispositions, and not upon our circumstances. Martha Washington

66. A. Nile.

67. You see children know such a lot now, they soon don't believe in fairies, and every time a child says, "I don't believe in fairies," there is a fairy somewhere that falls down dead. Sir James Matthew Barrie, *Peter Pan*

68. Four or three.

69. Slow but steady wins the race. Aesop, *The Hare and the Tortoise*

70. It begins in Georgia and ends in Maine.

71. The Nile.

72. Enigma.

73. Forgive and forget (4-give and 4-get).

74. If you move your head slowly, the shape will ripple.

75. Wales.

76. If you read the sentence carefully in the triangle, you will notice "THE" is written twice.

77. Salt.

78. Pacific Ocean.

79. Round about, round about, lo and behold! Reel away, reel away, straw into gold! And round about the wheel went merrily; the work was quickly done, and the straw was all spun into gold. Jacob and Wilhelm Grimm, *Rumpelstiltskin*

80. All of the squares are the same shade of yellow.

81. All of the squares are the same shade of gray.

82. Yes, they are the same shade of black.

83. "Nibble, nibble, gnaw, Who is nibbling at my little house?" The children answered: "The wind, the wind, The heaven-born wind." Jacob and Wilhelm Grimm, *Hansel and Gretel*

84. After looking at the green bird and staring into the cage, you will see a faint red bird. The same will happen after looking at the red bird except the after-image will be green.

85. Up the airy mountain,
    Down the rushy glen,
    We daren't go a-hunting
    For fear of little men;
    We folk, good folk,
    Trooping all together,
    Green jacket, red cap,
    And white owl's feather!

    William Allingham, *The Fairies*

86.

DISCOVERY

87. The bottom gear would continue to spin as if both gears were circular.

88. Switzerland.

89. If you stack them vertically, the last letter of each word spells "treasure."

90. Formula. The last two letters of all words in Group One are U.S. postal abbreviations. "LA" is the abbreviation for Louisiana.

91. When the two largest pieces are exchanged, each small square that is cut by the diagonal line becomes a little bit higher than it is wide. This means that the large square is no longer a perfect square. It has increased in height by an area that is exactly equal to the area of the 1X1 hole.

92. Amazon River.

93. Anchor.

94. They are all anagrams of "Father's Day."

95. The answer is 4 (add the spots around the corners of the dice that have a center spot).

96.

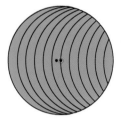

97. When you turn the W upside down it gives us an M. Now the word LLAMA can be spelled.

98.

99.

100.

101.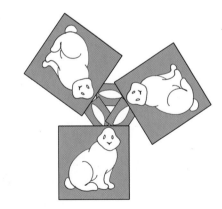

Acknowledgments

I would like to gratefully thank the following for material used in this book:

Nazca Line photographs, page 33, used with permission of Philip Baird/www.anthroarcheart.org

Ryan Brenizer for photographs of the Adirondack region, pages 10, 16

The Perry-Castañeda Library Map Collection, The University of Texas at Austin

Daniel Shearer for photographs of Greenwich, CT, pages 2, 24, 27, and Maui, HI, page 29

NASA for satellite images used on pages 32, 36

Clipart.com

En.wikipedia.org